THE PURPOSE OF HANDS

allison joseph

GLASS LYRE PRESS

Paperback ISBN: 978-1-941783-26-9

Cover art: Photonics | Dreamstime.com
Author Photo: Rusty Bailey
Design & layout: Steven Asmussen
Copyediting: Linda E. Kim

Glass Lyre Press, LLC
P.O. Box 2693
Glenview, IL 60026
www.GlassLyrePress.com

contents

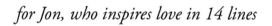

for Jon, who inspires love in 14 lines

WHY I CAN'T SWIM

If waves could wash away my sins in life—
the indiscretions, errors, and the blight,
my caustic words, the bitter need to fight
and rail against myself, reluctant wife
and never-mother, selfish woman, writer rife
with insecurities about the white
and black of this world, the grades of dark in light,
then I would learn to swim, embrace that strife.
But waves will only sink me to the floor
of any ocean, river, lake or pool
until I learn to hold my breath and dive
beneath the churning surfaces, demanding more
and better from myself, become a woman who'll
inhale, jump in, begin to thrash, then thrive.

SOMETHING SHE CAN FEEL

I've given up on beauty I can buy,
on tubes of paint for lips and eyes and face,
on eyelash curlers, curling irons, rows
of pencils, potions, powders. No bows
from my close-cropped hair, no caustic lye
to straighten out my kinks, deny my race.
I've turned instead to beauty I can feel:
the strength still in my limbs to pull or lift,
to walk until my brain begins to fire
the phrasing of the imagery required
to make a poem worth what it reveals,
not language gone astray, awry, adrift.
No glossy magazine will bring me peace—
only words—revised, refined—can bring release.

STITCHING

I want to stitch a poem I can wear
as loosely as a faded summer dress
that's fragile but still colorful, the best
that I can offer up, my shoulders bare
but warm beneath the sun, my skin aware
of languid August heat, but not oppressed
by humid reveries, the season's stress
not stunning me until I cease to care.
But I can't sew a garment out of words
until I know their textures inside out,
learn how to work their threads—the silky ones
that move like satin over limbs, assured
and sleek, the strident ones that clash and shout.
I'll stitch them all with finger, pen, and thumb.

Typographical

A comma hints at something more to come,
a colon says a list is starting up:
a run of names, of people that you loved,
of all the habits all those people stopped.
A period can put an end to thought,
though if you triple one, something's been cut
or something's trailing off. A question's not
a question 'til you end it with that mutt
of punctuation, odd curving mark, disjoint
as if it's questioning itself, its job
of inquiry. And an exclamation point's
obscene, so phallic with its single throb!
But semi-colons—they know compromise;
the clauses that they join, those will survive.

CRAZY

I love your every molecule and cell,
your mitochondria and DNA,
the wrinkles in your skin, the way they play
around your eyes and mouth. I love you well
and healthy in your gait; I love you ill
and sickly in my arms, your skin gone gray.
I love your limbs and muscles in their play,
your sweaty trembling in earthly chill.

But I won't love you better when you're dead,
won't find maturity in grief and pain,
resorting to my infancy instead
of mourning with restraint. I won't be sane
when you are taken from our marriage bed,
your skin to never liven it again.

Endure

Come crisis time, my hair won't be in place,
the bags beneath my eyes will swell like sacks.
No lipsticked smile stays plastered on my face
when favorite uncles die from heart attacks,
when aunts go frail from cancers in their breasts.
I lie awake, tight muscles in my back
so taut they ache and knot. Deep in my chest,
there's heaviness so dense it won't go slack
with water and some pills. My heart won't rest.
The wakes, the graves, my cache of mounting fears
don't dissipate at therapy's request,
anxieties increasing with my years.
But I'll endure, despite each mortal flaw,
alive's better than dead, though grief thrives, raw.

Such Sweet Sorrow

In Spanish, adios, in French, adieu,
so many ways to part, to mean farewell.
The origin of bye? *God be with you*
was the full phrase, a kind of verbal spell
that kept beloved ones away from harm
when travelling beyond our reach, our sight.
Now goodbye's lost that meaning, not a charm
we say to keep them safe throughout the night.
Goodbye is now a word we're loath to say,
its curt finality a slamming door
that might not open up again. The day
I breathe goodbye to you, I'll hope that more
than this mere word will bind us as our lives
conclude. Goodbye outlasts us all, survives.

EDUCATIONS

I used to be the smartest kid in class,
beloved by teachers for my reading skills,
obedience, my lack of sulky sass,
the way I loved vocabulary drills,
all tests of verbal aptitude. I'd read
the book assigned, then ask for more, content
as words grew bigger, more complex, freed
from numbing tales of Jane and Dick, my bent
toward talking animals and space. But now
I'm standing up in front of them to teach,
expecting admiration as I show
how far their words can come, who they can reach.
The smartest kid in class now strives for clues
about these shifty words, all they can do.

FAITHFUL

I'm flawed, I'm flawed, I'm flawed, I'm flawed, I'm flawed
goes the refrain that sings inside my head.
When will this self-doubt end—when I am dead,
my body done with highs and lows, seesaw
of emotions kaput? Such feelings gnaw
at intellect's good will, until I dread
awakening to face the day ahead,
self-confidence as vulnerable as straw.
But then I hear my husband calling me,
his voice accepting everything I am:
the woman flawed, the better mind within
her doubt, her nervous personality.
I rise and know my life is not a sham—
where doubt leaves off, his love for me begins.

KNOWLEDGE

Encyclopedias can't tell me truth
and dictionaries cannot make me weep.
An atlas cannot help me find the way
beyond beliefs I swore were right in youth.
My questions keep me stirring in my sleep:
how life begins and how it's going to end,
which prophets to believe and which to shun,
which heaven hears the prayers in my breath,
and should I walk upright, or kneel and bend?
Which answers have validity, which none?
Such questions are the only means to grow—
no reference book can help me find a faith,
no answers come to me in graphs and charts.
The more I know, the more I do not know.

BLANK

An empty page once ready to be filled,
an empty glass, no wine to tempt my tongue.
A vacant lot, no house on weed-strewn land,
no gardens yet to reap, no rows to till.
No arias, not art songs to be sung,
no amplified guitar or clapping hands.
No blown glass beads or silver hammered thin
adorning ears or throats. No violins
or harps, no chamber groups or bebop bands,
no books with wisdom tucked somewhere within.
That's what this world would be if you were dead,
no longer in my arms but gone to earth,
beyond my touch and reach of any word.
Without you here, there's nothing in my head.

PMS

You summon me from sleep to feel your grip,
demand that I remember that my womb
is more than just an empty space for lease,
more than a parking lot or vacant room
in need of renovation. I'm in my slip
and panties, bent double, hoping for release
from your nagging, haggling woman-pain I know
won't be the death of me, just of my ease
at living in this body. I hug my hips,
curl in a ball as if to fend off blows,
massage my achy back with both my palms.
The more I toss, the more your aching grows.
In beds around the globe, we're cursing, blue,
our heating pads turned up to vanquish you.

Beware of Self

How can a clumsy woman be redeemed?
Must every knife be hidden from her grasp,
all clothing triple-stitched in every seam,
hot liquids served in heat-resistant glass?
How can we save her from this prickly world
of shattered glass on sidewalks, oil slicks—
a world that's tripped her since she was a girl?
Potholes and pointy tables do their tricks
to twist her, bruise her, break her timid stride;
she's learned to brace herself on the way down,
to tell herself that there's no loss of pride
when getting up from falling to the ground.
Redeem me with a hand to steady me;
brush off the dirt while others rush to flee.

On Womanhood

The ache of womanhood hardly relents,
subsiding only when we leave this life.
The ache of spinsterhood, of being wife
to everyone and nobody presents
small chance for us to grow, to re-invent
each self. The ache of motherhood's a knife
that cuts us deep in tenderness and strife,
in knowledge of the harm we can't prevent.
But the ache of being woman has its joys:
the womb a palace nothing else can match,
one cord connecting life to blood and back.
New flesh can thrive within, and then detach,
thrust whole into the world, not yet destroyed
by all this world's affronts, defeats, attacks.

Expletive

I don't say it a lot but when I do,
I relish each explosive bit of sound:
the "f" that kicks its way out of my mouth,
announcing nothing anyone can say
will change my mood, that sulky letter "u"
that puckers up my pouting lips around
this fine obscenity, the "c" uncouth,
colliding into "k"—get out its way.
The word shoots right on out of you
before propriety can force it down,
too audibly revealing hidden truths,
the angers that we fail to keep at bay.
Console me if you hear that word from me—
something big's awry. You'd better come see.

PETITION

Please let me do extraordinary work
creating poetry, all that implies.
Give me the strength to write through my own lies,
persist through my own laziness, not shirk
from what I fear, those necessary quirks
than make me less than great, not wise
but human still. Let inspirations rise
until I cannot stop; don't let me smirk
at my own cleverness. Make me a source
of what makes sense, not just what's beautiful,
though make it beautiful enough to sing.
Some call you God. I know you as the voice
that pushes me through pain to bountiful
mistakes, alive in spite of everything.

THE DISAPPEARED

The voices that you'll never hear again
can haunt you by their very lack of sound—
a stillness unlike anything around,
a silence underneath the noise of men
and women, hush that serves as requiem
for those we've lost, a quiet void profound
in its grief. If only voices could be bound,
kept wrapped away within, padlocked and penned.
But letters that the dead have left behind—
their phrases, inked in broad uncertain scrawls
or tiny mannered print, the words they wrote—
are evidence that language can remind
us what we need to know, how to recall
those voices, once unheard, become remote.

The Purpose of Hands

An open palm can mean hello; a fist
can mean goodbye. A single finger crooked,
moved back and forth, can lead you to a kiss—
or slap. A finger pointed down will make you look
down too, to ponder what's beneath your shoes—
that hell you've heard about, or someplace else?
A finger pointing heavenward's a ruse
to make us all behave, aware the self's
under a cosmic microscope. We point
at those we fear, at those we scorn, at those
we single out in pride or shame. We taunt
with middle fingers held up high. We pose
with hands across our hearts to swear our trust.
We speak with hands, not words, because we must.

MODERN MATURITY

My knees don't buckle when I think of you;
I don't go weak whenever you walk by.
No quiver in my gut, my palms stay dry,
no chattering about a rendezvous
to come. No tears when you bid me adieu;
I don't go on and on about your eyes.
I don't think loving you will make the sky
much brighter than its daily sullen blue.

My love for you runs deeper than the claims
of ingénues and starlets, than the trends
in books that state all marriages are doomed
to flare up fast, then burn out quick. My aim?
To share a solid love that doesn't bend,
a love where we are fed, but not consumed.

ONE

Just one of everything is all I need—
one bed to rest my weary body in,
one body to defile with mortal sin,
one mouth I open up to taste, to feed
on anything that fuels my meager speed,
my achy limbs. One nose, one stubby chin
that trembles if I stutter, pout, or win,
one heart that swells to beat and then recedes.
But then again, I've got two failing eyes
that strain to see what's shadowed in the dim
light before dawn. These eyes are all I've got
to take your image in, to know the wise
wrinkles around your eyes. I've got four limbs
to grasp you closer in, love what you're not.

ABOUT THE AUTHOR

Allison Joseph lives, writes, and teaches in Carbondale Illinois, where she is part of the creative writing faculty at Southern Illinois University. She serves as editor and poetry editor of *Crab Orchard Review*, moderator of the Creative Writers Opportunities List, and director of the Young Writers Workshop, a summer writers' workshop for teen writers.

Her books and chapbooks include *What Keeps Us Here* (Ampersand Press), *Soul Train* (Carnegie Mellon University Press), *In Every Seam* (University of Pittsburgh Press), *Worldly Pleasures* (Word Tech Communications), *Imitation of Life* (Carnegie Mellon UP), *Voice: Poems* (Mayapple Press), *My Father's Kites* (Steel Toe Books), *Trace Particles* (Backbone Press), *Little Epiphanies* (Imaginary Friend Press), *Mercurial* (Mayapple Press), *Mortal Rewards* (White Violet Press), *Multitudes* (Word Poetry), *Corporal Muse* (Yellow Chair Press), *Double Identity* (Singing Bone Press), and *What Once You Loved* (Barefoot Muse Press). She is the literary partner and wife of poet and editor Jon Tribble.

Glass Lyre Press

exceptional works to replenish the spirit

Glass Lyre Press is an independent literary publisher interested in technically accomplished, stylistically distinct, and original work. Glass Lyre seeks diverse writers that possess a dynamic aesthetic and an ability to emotionally and intellectually engage a wide audience of readers.

Glass Lyre's vision is to connect the world through language and art. We hope to expand the scope of poetry and short fiction for the general reader through exceptionally well-written books, which evoke emotion, provide insight, and resonate with the human spirit.

Poetry Collections
Poetry Chapbooks
Select Short & Flash Fiction
Anthologies

www.GlassLyrePress.com

CPSIA information can be obtained
at www.ICGtesting.com
Printed in the USA
BVHW07s1711020818
523375BV00001B/77/P